DAD
JOKES

DAD JOKES

GROAN-WORTHY QUIPS, PUNS,
AND ALMOST-FUNNY GAGS

A. GRAMBS

**UNION
SQUARE
& CO.**

NEW YORK

UNION
SQUARE
& CO.

NEW YORK

UNION SQUARE & CO. and the distinctive Union Square & Co. logo
are registered trademarks of Sterling Publishing Co., Inc.

Union Square & Co., LLC, is a subsidiary of
Sterling Publishing Co., Inc.

ISBN 978-1-4549-4893-3
ISBN 978-1-4549-4894-0 (e-book)

For information about custom editions,
special sales, and premium purchases, please
contact specialsales@unionsquareandco.com.

Printed in Malaysia

2 4 6 8 10 9 7 5 3

unionsquareandco.com

Cover design by Igor Satanovsky
Interior design by Gavin Motnyk

CONTENTS

CHAPTER 1

ALL THINGS HUMAN

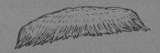

WHAT PLASTIC SURGERY DO OLD CONSTRUCTION WORKERS GET?

Fork-lifts.

WHY DO ANGELS HAVE BAD BREATH?

Chronic halo-tosis.

HOW DID CHIROPRACTORS PARTY IN THE 1970S?

They went herniated disc-o dancing.

WHY IS THE OPHTHALMOLOGIST IN THE HOSPITAL?

Eye don't know.

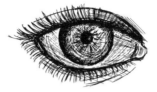

WHERE DO YOU STORE A LIVER, BLADDER, KIDNEYS, AND INTESTINES?

In an organ-izer.

WHAT PART OF THE BODY IS USED TO JOIN TWO SENTENCES?

The colon.

WHAT'S A GOOD NAME FOR AN EYE DOCTOR?

Iris.

HOW DID ALL THE BONES IN YOUR BODY MEET?

They joint a club.

WHAT'S THE COOLEST PART OF THE HUMAN BODY?

The hip.

WHY DID THE LEAF GO TO THE HOSPITAL?

It had a bad fall.

WHAT DID THE POOP EMOJI SAY ON *WHEEL OF FORTUNE*?

"I'll take a bowel, please."

WHAT DO PEOPLE WHO ARE SCARED OF FEET SUFFER FROM?

Lac-toes intolerance.

WHY ISN'T THE NOSE STILL RUNNING?

Because it came up to a STOP sinus.

HOW COULD THE CORONER TELL THE PASTA CHEF WAS DEAD?

Rigor-toni mortis had set in.

WHAT IS THE KEY TO BECOMING A SUCCESSFUL DOCTOR?

A lot of patients.

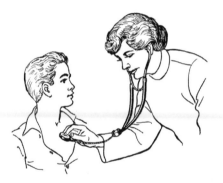

WHAT'S A GOOD NAME FOR A MUGGER?

Rob.

WHAT KIND OF DENTIST WORKS IN THE MILITARY?

A drill sergeant.

WHAT METAL DO ROBBERS USE TO BREAK INTO HOUSES?

Steal.

WHAT'S A PARAMEDIC'S FAVORITE PLANT?

IV.

WHAT'S A GOOD NAME FOR A COOK?

Stu.

WHAT'S A GOOD NAME FOR A LAWYER?

Sue.

HOW DID THE LOBSTER BECOME A LAWYER?

It went to claw school.

WHY DID THE JURY LAUGH AT THE LAWYER?

He was showing them his briefs.

WHAT DOES A LAWYER WEAR TO COURT?

A law suit.

WHAT GAME DO BANKS PLAY?

Check-ers.

WHAT'S A GOOD NAME FOR A WAITER?

Trey.

WHY DID THE WAITRESS QUIT HER JOB?

She didn't like taking orders.

HOW DO BANK ROBBERS GET AWAY FROM IT ALL?

In a get-away car.

WHY DID THE JANITOR GET FIRED?

He got caught sweeping on the job.

WHY WAS THE GARBAGE MAN CRYING?

Because he got canned.

WHAT'S A GOOD NAME FOR A KARAOKE SINGER?

Mike.

WHAT MAKES SOMEONE AN EXCELLENT BAKER?

They cater to your every knead.

WHO RESCUED THE DROWNING PUMPKIN?

The life-gourd.

HOW DO SAILORS SEND PACKAGES TO THEIR FAMILIES?

They ship them.

WHAT DO POLITICIANS SPREAD ON THEIR HAM SANDWICHES?

Mayor-naise.

HOW DOES A MAILMAN STOP A FIRE?

He stamps it out.

WHY DID THE WAITRESS CALL HER STOCKBROKER?

She was looking for a good tip.

MANAGER: HOW ARE SALES FOR THAT NEW PERFUME?

SALESWOMAN: Scent-sational!

HOW DO LADDERS HELP YOUR CAREER?

They give you a step up.

HOW DO EYEBALLS FIGHT?

They tend to lash out.

HOW DOES A COWBOY CATCH A HERD OF RUNAWAY EYEBALLS?

He lash-oes them.

WHAT SHOULD YOU WEAR ON YOUR LEGS AT A BASEBALL GAME?

Knee caps.

WHAT KIND OF CAR DOES A RICH KNEE DRIVE?

A Bent-ly.

WHAT HAPPENS IF YOU PARK YOUR FOOT IN ONE PLACE FOR TOO LONG?

It gets toe-d.

WHAT FISH SMELLS LIKE FEET?

Fillet of sole.

HOW COME THE FOOT WAS CONSIDERED A MIRACLE WORKER?

It had heel-ing powers.

WHAT'S A GOOD NAME FOR A FOOT?
Arch-ie.

WHAT'S ANOTHER GOOD NAME FOR A FOOT?
Toe-ny.

WHERE DO YOU CATCH COLDS?
On a choo-choo train.

WHAT DOES A KING'S SON ALWAYS LEAVE ON THE BEACH?
Foot-prince.

WHAT PART OF THE BODY MAKES A GOOD PASTA SAUCE?

The toe-mato.

WHAT DOES THE AUTOBIOGRAPHY OF A LEG TALK ABOUT?

Its thighs and lows.

WHY DID THE FORTUNE TELLER MOVE TO FLORIDA?

She needed more palms to read.

WHAT'S A GOOD WAY TO CARRY BARBECUED FOOD?

In a rib-cage.

HOW DOES A CHIN CROSS THE STREET?

First he looks right, then cleft.

WHAT'S A GOOD NAME FOR A GUY WITH A FURRY CHEST?

Harry.

WHAT'S A GOOD NAME FOR A BOY WITH A SHORT HAIRCUT?

Bob.

WHAT MAGAZINE DO GARDENERS LIKE TO READ?

Weeder's Digest.

WHAT'S A NOSE'S FAVORITE COLOR?

Blew.

WHY WAS THE NOSE SO POOR?

It didn't have a scent to its name.

HOW DID THE COLD SPREAD?

It flu.

WHY DOESN'T THE CHIN LIKE THE NOSE?

The chin thinks the nose is stuffy.

WHY DID THE SHIP SNEEZE?

It had a mast-y cold.

WHY DID THE COW STAY HOME WITH A COLD?

She was milking it for all it was worth.

WHAT KIND OF SHOTS DO SICK HUNTERS FIRE WHEN THEY GO HUNTING?

Flu shots.

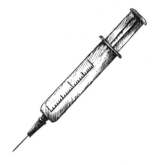

WHY DID THE COMPUTER STAY HOME FROM SCHOOL?

It had a virus.

HOW CAN YOU TELL YOUR NECK IS ANGRY?

You've got a sore throat.

WHAT ALLERGY MAKES HORSES SNEEZE?

Hay fever.

WHAT PART OF YOUR BODY CAN FINISH A MARATHON?

Your runny nose.

HOW COME THE MAN IS ALWAYS BURPING?

He works at a gas station.

BUNNY: HEY, DOC, HOW BAD IS IT?

DOCTOR: Well, you've got a hare-line fracture.

WHY COULDN'T THE FOOT AFFORD TO BUY A NEW SHOE?

Because it was broke.

HOW DID THE DOCTOR TELL HER PATIENT HE BROKE HIS FOOT?

She braced him for the bad news.

WHAT INJURY DO BULLFIGHTERS GET?

Spain-ed ankles.

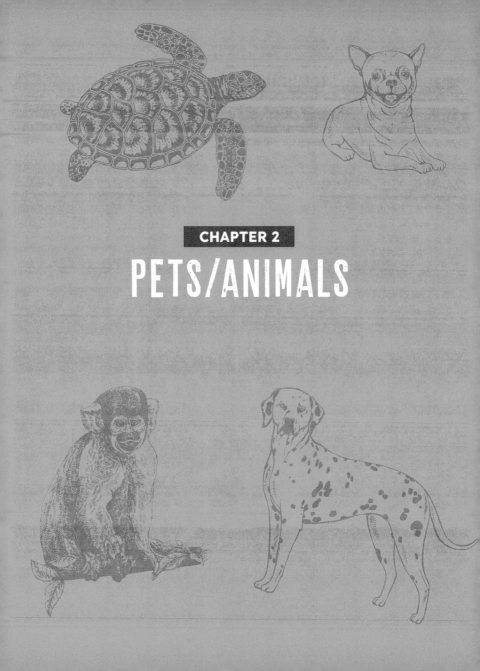

CHAPTER 2

PETS/ANIMALS

WHAT DO MONKEYS SIP TO CELEBRATE AN ANNIVERSARY?

Chimp-agne.

SHARKS BROADCAST THE NIGHTLY NEWS HOW?

They live feed-ing frenzy it!

WHY DO COWS NEED PUBLICISTS ON A RANCH?
To market their brand.

LOVEBUGS ON YOUR WINDSHIELD ARE CALLED WHAT?
A roadside attraction.

ON WHAT DATING SHOW DID THE GERMAN SHEPHERD MEET THE SIBERIAN HUSKY?
90-Day Fleancé.

WHAT HOURS DOES A SERVICE DOG WORK?

Oh, usually ca-nine to five.

WHAT DID THE FAST-FOOD DRIVE-THRU-WINDOW OPERATOR SAY TO THE SKUNK?

"Hi, can I take your odor?"

HOW DO AUSTRALIAN BIRDS SHOW THEY ARE HAPPY?

They send each other smiley-face emujis.

WHAT SPECIALIST CURES ELEPHANTS OF THEIR ACNE?

A pachydermatologist.

WHERE DOES AN ORNITHOLOGIST JOT DOWN HER HOPES AND DREAMS?

On her vision bird, duh!

KNOCK KNOCK.
Who's there?
SAFARI.
Safari who?

Safari . . . and yet so close.

HOW DO INSECTS RESEARCH THEIR GENEALOGY?

They sign up for Antcestry.com.

WHAT FARM ANIMAL IS THE GREATEST OF ALL TIME?

The G.O.A.T.

WHAT OCEAN VESSEL IS FULL OF CRYBABIES?

A whale-ing ship.

HOW DOES A SCALY MAMMAL KNOW WHEN TO EAT?

When it's experiencing hunger pangolins.

SEABIRDS EAT WHAT FOR BREAKFAST EVERY MORNING?

Bagulls with cream cheese.

WHAT ENERGY SNACKS DO CHIMPS LIKE?

Monkey bars.

HOW DO BULLS DRIVE THEIR CARS?

With steer-ing wheels.

WHY ARE BABY GOATS FUN TO PLAY WITH?

They're always kidding around.

WHY ARE FISH EASY TO FOOL?

Because they're so gill-able.

WHICH SEA CREATURES WORK OUT AT THE GYM?

Mussels.

WHAT KIND OF SWEATERS DO TORTOISES WEAR?

Turtle-necks.

HOW CAN YOU TELL THAT A WHALE IS SAD?

By its blubber-ing.

WHY DID THE ESCARGOT VISIT THE MANICURE SALON?

She needed to get her snails done.

WHAT'S A GOOD NAME FOR AN OYSTER?

Pearl.

WHAT DO FISHERMEN DO AT A CLASSICAL MUSIC CONCERT?

Tuna piano.

WHAT DID THE SEA LION DO BEFORE MAILING HIS LETTER?

Seal the envelope.

WHERE DO PIGS SLEEP IN THE SUMMERTIME?

In ham-mocks.

WHAT PREHISTORIC ANIMALS EAT IN COFFEE SHOPS?

Diner-saurs.

HOW DID THE CROCODILE GET TO THE TOP OF THE BUILDING?

He took the ele-gator.

WHAT'S A GOOD NAME FOR A GRIZZLY BEAR?

Teddy.

WHAT'S A GOOD NAME FOR A DUCK?

Bill.

WHAT BIRD WEARS A TOUPEE?

A bald eagle.

WHY IS IT SO HARD TO MOVE A PARAKEET?
Because they don't budge-y for anyone.

WHAT BIRD LIVES IN YOUR THROAT?
A swallow.

WHY DIDN'T THE DUCK LIKE TO GO OUT TO DINNER?
It always got stuck with the bill.

HOW DO FELINES CARRY THEIR MONEY?
In cat-nap sacks.

WHAT'S A SCIENTIST'S FAVORITE DOG?

The Lab.

WHAT DOG IS THE BEST SWIMMER?

A lap dog.

WHAT DO YOU GIVE A DOG TO MAKE HIM LAUGH?

A funny bone.

WHAT INSECT IS A GOOD LETTER-WRITER?

A spelling bee.

WHAT IS A MATADOR'S FAVORITE DOG?

The bulldog.

WHY DIDN'T THE DOG GET CAUGHT STEALING THE BONE?

Because he flea-ed the scene before the
cops showed up.

WHAT DO DVRs AND DOGS HAVE IN COMMON?

They both have pause.

WHAT ANIMAL MAKES THE BEST BUTLER?

A go-pher.

WHAT POLICE UNIT DO FLIES FEAR MOST?

The SWAT team.

WHERE DID THE HORSE GO FOR DINNER?

To his neigh-bor's house.

WHAT DO DOGS FEAR MOST AT THE VET?

Getting a cat-scan.

CHAPTER 3

FOOD

WHY DID THE SALAD BLEED OUT?

Its carrot-id artery got chopped.

WHAT CULINARY EXPERT IS ALWAYS IN LITIGATION?

A sous chef.

HOW DOES A SCOOP OF ICE CREAM BEGIN JOURNALING?

"Dear Dairy . . ."

WHERE DOES A BAKER GO WHEN HE DIES?

Into the Afterloaf.

WHAT KIND OF EGG HESITATES TOO MUCH?

An um . . . um . . . um-let.

WHAT KIND OF CHEESE DID MEDUSA LOVE?

Gorgon-zola.

WHY DO BARISTAS' ROMANTIC RELATIONSHIPS NEVER LAST?

Because they have trouble espresso-ing their feelings.

WHERE DO COOKS GO TO TRADE CHICKEN SOUP RECIPES?

The New York Stock Exchange.

WHAT FRUIT MAKES DRINKING EASIER?

The straw-berry.

WHAT FOOD IS ALWAYS TRIPPING?

Falafel.

. . . AND WHERE DOES IT ALWAYS FALL?

Into a pit-a.

WHAT DO POETS POUR ON THEIR CEREAL IN THE MORNING?

Odemilk.

WHY DID THE CAPPUCCINO MOVE TO HOLLYWOOD?

He wanted to become foam-ous.

WHY IS YOGURT DISAPPEARING FROM GROCERY STORE SHELVES?

Cancel culture.

WHAT VEGETABLE DOESN'T DO WELL ON ROLLER COASTERS?

The puke-cumber.

HOW DO YOU COOK PASTA WHILE MAKING A CALL?

Use a burner phone.

WHY COULDN'T THE ITALIAN PASTA START THE CAR?

It had gnocchi.

WHAT ROOT VEGETABLES CAN TELL YOUR FUTURE?

Taro cards.

WHY DID THE GRAPEFRUIT GET KICKED OUT OF THE CHORUS?

He kept hitting sour notes.

HOW DO YOU GET TWO FRUITS TO DANCE?

You pear them up.

WHAT HAPPENS WHEN A GRAPE IS GETTING OLD AND CRANKY?

It starts to wine.

WHAT FRUIT UNLOCKS DOORS?

The ki-wi.

WHY DID THE BANANA GET A SPEEDING TICKET?

He got caught peeling out of the parking lot.

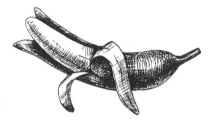

WHAT'S A GOOD NAME FOR A FRUIT?

Barry.

WHY DID THE POLICE PHOTOGRAPH THE CUP OF COFFEE?

To get its mug shot.

WHAT DRINK MAKES YOU GO "OUCH!"?

Punch.

WHAT TYPES OF JOKES DO FARMERS MAKE?

Corn-y ones.

LEM: HEY, DID YOU HEAR ABOUT THE NEW ANIMATED MOVIE ABOUT THE PRINCESS WHO FALLS IN LOVE WITH A VEGETABLE FARMER?

CLEM: Yup, it's called *Beauty and the Beets*.

WHAT DID THE CARROT HOPE FOR ON ITS VACATION?

Peas and quiet.

HOW DO YOU SEND A BOUQUET TO SOMEONE ON MOTHER'S DAY?

You caul-i-flower shop.

WHAT'S THE MOST ADORABLE VEGETABLE IN THE FIELD?

The cute-cumber.

WHAT VEGETABLE IS KEPT IN A CAGE?

A zoo-chini.

WHY WAS THE LETTUCE A BIG SUCCESS?

He had a head for business.

HOW DO YOU GET A PIECE OF BREAD TO DO YOU A FAVOR?

You butter it up.

WHAT DO YOU CALL A SOUTHWESTERN DISH THAT'S BEEN IN THE FREEZER?

A burrrr-ito.

HOW DO LOAVES OF BREAD CONGRATULATE EACH OTHER?

With a toast.

WHAT IS A SAILOR'S FAVORITE SANDWICH?

A sub.

WHAT IS A SOLDIER'S FAVORITE SANDWICH?

The hero.

WHY DOES BREAD GET FAT?

Because it loafs around all day.

WHAT EGG WEARS COWBOY BOOTS?

A Western omelet.

WHAT NOISE DO STOLEN HAMBURGERS SET OFF?

Burger alarms.

WHAT'S A CLOCK'S FAVORITE MEAL?

Minute steak.

WHAT KIND OF PASTA HAS LOTS OF PIMPLES?

Zit-i.

WHAT'S A GOOD SNACK TO EAT ON FATHER'S DAY?

Pop-corn.

WHY COULDN'T THE EGG GET GOOD RECEPTION ON HIS TELEVISION?

All the channels were scrambled.

WHAT'S A GOOD NAME FOR AN EGG?

Shelley.

WHAT DO YOU EAT FOR LUNCH IN A CEMETERY?

Tomb-atoes and grave-y.

WHY DON'T DETECTIVES MAKE GOOD VEGETARIANS?

Because they're always on steak-outs.

HOW DO YOU KNOW WHEN SEAFOOD MAKES YOU SICK?

Your skin gets clammy.

WHAT'S A GOOD NAME FOR A HOT DOG?

Frank.

WHAT'S A GOOD NAME FOR A HAMBURGER?

Patty.

WHAT LANGUAGE DO COLD CUTS SPEAK?

Spam-ish.

WHERE DOES SPAGHETTI GO TO DANCE?

To a meat-ball.

WHICH SANDWICH TASTES BEST AT THE BEACH?

Peanut butter and jelly-fish.

ON WHICH DAY OF THE WEEK DOES ICE CREAM TASTE BEST?

Sundae.

WHAT DESSERT HELPS YOU DRINK YOUR MILK?

Cup-cakes.

HOW DOES A PIECE OF PIE SEE THE FUTURE?

Through a crust-al ball.

WHAT CANDY SHRINKS WHEN YOU PUT IT IN THE DRYER?

Cotton candy.

WHAT HAPPENS IF YOU PUT TOO MANY COCOA BEANS IN YOUR MOUTH?

You choke-a-lot.

WHAT DO SWEET OLD LADIES WALK WITH?

Sugar canes.

WHAT LANGUAGE DO PASTRIES SPEAK?

Danish.

WHAT DO BALLOONS DRINK AT BIRTHDAY PARTIES?

Soda pop.

WHAT CANDY DO TEETH LOVE MOST?

Gum-my bears.

WHAT DO POOR SQUIRRELS HUNT FOR IN THE WINTER?

Dough-nuts.

WHAT TREAT DO THEY SERVE IN PRISON?

Jail-y doughnuts.

CHAPTER 4

TECH

WHAT DO YOU BRING TO A SOFTWARE ENGINEER'S SURPRISE PARTY?

A birthday gif, of course!

HOW DOES THE POPE BUY SOMETHING ON E-BAY?

He uses Pa-pal.

HOW DO TEA CUPS RAISE MONEY FOR CHARITY?

Crowd-saucering.

WHAT DO INSTAGRAMMERS EAT ON ST. PATRICK'S DAY?

Corned beef hash-tag.

WHAT SOCIAL MEDIA PLATFORM SPREADS LYME DISEASE?

TickTok.

HOW DOES A DAD RAISE MONEY FOR HIS JOKE TELLING?

He starts a GoPunMe page!

HOW DO HACKERS RELAX ON VACATION?

They go phishing.

. . . AND WHAT DO THEY USE TO CATCH THOSE PHISH?

Clickbait.

HOW DO LOBSTERS BROADCAST THEIR FUNERALS?

They live-steam it.

HOW DID THE PSYCHIC MEDIUM BREAK UP WITH HER BOYFRIEND ON SOCIAL MEDIA?

She ghosted him.

WHAT DID THE GIRL GIF SAY TO THE BOY GIF WHEN SHE DUMPED HIM?

"It's not you, it's meme."

WHERE DO BABY CHICKS POST THEIR SELFIES?

On Fuzzbook.

HOW DO BIRDS COMMUNICATE ONLINE?

They tweet.

HOW DO SPIDERS EARN ONLINE DEGREES?

They sign up for Webinars.

WHAT DO YOU CALL TERMITES ADVERTISING ON A WEBSITE?

Sponsored pests.

WHAT KIND OF MONEY IS BURIED?

Crypt-ocurrency.

WHAT TYPE OF MONEY GIVES YOU RABIES?

Bit-coin.

WHY ARE INFORMATION TECHNOLOGISTS SUCH LOUSY DANCERS?

Because they've got no algo-rithm.

WHAT DOES AN EBAYER SELL?
Oh, a little bid of this and a little bid of that.

HOW DO HEAVYWEIGHT HACKERS BEAT EACH OTHER UP?
In doxing matches.

WHY DO CHIMNEYS GET SO MANY LIKES ON INSTAGRAM?
Because they're effective social media in-flue-ncers.

WHY DO SPIDERS ENJOY COMPUTERS SO MUCH?

They like to play on the web.

WHY WAS THE RESTAURANT OWNER HAVING A TOUGH TIME GETTING HIS WEBSITE RUNNING?

Because he didn't have a good server.

WHY DID THE COMPUTER SCREEN GET IN TROUBLE WITH HIS MOTHER?

Because he was a cursor.

HOW DO FLOWERS STAY IN TOUCH ON THE INTERNET?

With their bud-dy lists.

COMPUTERS ENJOY WHAT POPULAR SNACK?

Chips and dip.

HOW DO YOU KEEP A COMPUTER'S BREATH FRESH?

Give it a docu-mint.

HOW DO FINGERS COMMUNICATE ON A COMPUTER?

By e-nail.

HOW DID THE POLICE OFFICER STOP THE RUNAWAY REFRIGERATOR?

She yelled "Freeze!"

WHAT KIND OF SHIRT DOES A COMPUTER WEAR TO SCHOOL?

A lap-top.

WHY DID ONE FONT DUMP THE OTHER FONT?

He wasn't her type.

WHAT IS THE NEW WAY TO CURE A SICK COMPUTER?

Treat it with modem medicine.

WHY DID THE COMPUTER CALL THE EXTERMINATOR?

It had a mouse.

HOW DO COMPUTERS GET PLACED IN HONORS CLASSES?

They go through a screen-ing process.

WHERE DO DVDS LIKE TO VACATION?

In remote islands.

HOW DO YOU BORROW A CAMERA?

Someone lens it to you.

WHICH STEREOS GIVE THE FINEST LECTURES?

The ones with the best speakers!

WHY DID THE OLD-FASHIONED CAMERA FIND THE DIGITAL CAMERA SO ANNOYING?

Because she was always talking and he couldn't shutter up!

WHICH TELEVISION SHOWS ARE THE CLEANEST?

Soaps.

WHERE DID THE CAMERA TAKE HIS DATE?

To a film.

WHY AREN'T PHOTOGRAPHERS FUN TO HAVE AROUND?

Because of their negative attitudes.

WHAT DO PHONE STORES DO?

They cell phones, duh!

WHAT DO PHONES EXCHANGE WHEN THEY GET MARRIED?

Rings.

HOW DO PRISONERS STAY IN TOUCH WITH EACH OTHER?

With their cell phones.

HOW DO YOU GET OFF THE PHONE WITH A CLOSET?

You hang up.

WHY DO SURGEONS GET SO MANY PHONE CALLS?

Because they're big operators.

WHY WAS THE COMPUTER WEARING A MUZZLE?

So it wouldn't byte.

WHAT HAPPENED AT THE FOOTBALL GAME BETWEEN THE CELL PHONES AND THE CORDLESS PHONES?

The ref made a bad call.

WHAT DO YOU SEND A TELEPHONE WHEN IT'S ONE YEAR OLD?

A birthday cord.

WAS THE COMPUTER'S ROAD TRIP TO CALIFORNIA FUN?

Yes, but it was a hard drive.

HOW DO YOU GET A BOOK TO COME TO THE TELEPHONE?

You page it.

WHERE DO MOST TELEPHONES LIVE?

In Connect-icut.

WHAT'S THE BEST WAY TO GET IN TOUCH WITH YOUR MOTHER?

Ring-er.

WHAT'S A GOOD NAME FOR AN ATM?

Rich.

WHY DO YOU NEED AN ATM TO MAKE PIZZA?

That's where you get the dough, silly!

CHAPTER 5
TRAVEL

HOW DO YOU KNOW WHEN A FLAN HAS BEEN ARRESTED IN SPAIN?

Police take it into custard-y.

WHAT DID THE DOCTOR GIVE TO HIS CZECHOSLOVAKIAN PATIENT?

A good Prague-nosis!

DAUGHTER: "DAD, CAN WE GO TO NORWAY FOR VACATION?"

DAD: "Sorry, honey. We can't afjord it."

WHY DID THE TSA AGENT START SEEING A THERAPIST?

She was dealing with a lot of baggage and didn't think she could carry-on.

WHEN DID THE TOURIST'S ALLERGIES START ACTING UP?

The moment she arrived at her vacation dust-ination.

WHAT DID THE CUSTOMS AGENT SAY AT THE DINNER TABLE?

"Pass-port the salt, please."

WHAT DO YOU CALL IT WHEN A DAD WEARS THE WRONG CLOTHES AT A FASHION SHOW IN PARIS?

A fashion faux papa.

WHAT DO YOU CALL AN UNFRIENDLY HOTEL?

A hostel.

WHAT AFRICAN COUNTRY DO DROIDS VISIT FOR VACATION?

Ro-Botswana.

WHERE DOES EVERY UNCLE TREK TO FIND A WIFE?

Antarctica.

HOW DOES A SWIMMER QUENCH HER THIRST IN THE ATLANTIC OCEAN?

She takes a Gulp of Mexico.

HOW DO YOU ORDER A MEATBALL HERO IN ITALY?

Use sub-titles.

WHAT MEDITERRANEAN FOOD SINGS WHILE YOU EAT IT?

Hummus.

WHAT ANNUAL RACE DO FRENCH WAITERS COMPETE IN?

The Grand Prix Fixe.

WHAT'S THE BEST WAY TO CARRY A FRESH LOAF OF BREAD IN PARIS?

You bag-uette.

WHAT MEAL GIVES EUROPEAN TOURISTS THE RUNS?

The incontinent-al breakfast.

KNOCK KNOCK.
Who's there?
MISERY.
Misery who?

Misery is next to Kansas!

HOW CAN YOU TELL A FRENCHMAN IS SHOCKED?
He shouts out, "Lord have merci!"

WHAT DOES A WAITER DO AT THE BEACH?
He surfs food.

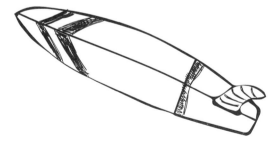

WHAT'S THE WRONG PLACE TO STAY ON A VACATION?

An err B&B.

WHAT DOES A BEACH GHOST SAY?

"Buoy!"

WHAT'S A GOOD NAME FOR THE SUN?

Ray.

WHY WAS THE SURFER DUDE YAWNING AT THE BEACH?

Because he was board.

WHAT DO CLAMS DO WHEN IT RAINS AT THE BEACH?

They seek shell-ter.

WHY DID THE OCEAN'S MOTHER PUNISH HIM?

Because he wasn't keeping his room tide-y.

WHAT DO FISHING BOATS DO WHEN THEY CATCH THE FLU?

They make an appointment with the local dock.

WHAT DOES A TROPICAL FRUIT WEAR TO THE BEACH?

A bikiwi.

WHAT BIKINI GOT STUCK IN A CHIMNEY?

The bathing soot.

WHAT DID THE KNEECAP GET WHEN IT WENT SCUBA DIVING?

The bends.

WHAT DO ELEPHANTS WEAR TO THE BEACH?

Trunks.

WHAT DO HAMBURGERS DO AT THE BEACH?

Build bun-fires.

WHERE DO MOVIE STARS VACATION?

On a Tom Cruise ship.

HOW DOES SEAWEED MOVE?

With a little kelp from its friends.

WHAT DOES THE OCEAN SPREAD AT CHRISTMASTIME?

Good tide-ings.

WHY WAS THE OCEAN A LOUSY HOUSE GUEST?

Because it made a lot of long-distance foam calls.

WHAT DOES THE OCEAN DO TO SAY GOODBYE?

Wave.

WHY DID THE SUN GET STRAIGHT A'S?

Because it was very bright.

HOW DID THE CHIMNEY SWEEP GET TO CALIFORNIA?

He flue on a plane.

HOW DID THE PILOT FLY WITHOUT DIRECTIONS?

He just winged it.

WHY DID THE HELICOPTER TURN AROUND IN MID-FLIGHT?

It felt propelled to do so.

WHAT DID THE COW JUMP OVER?

The moooooo-n.

WHAT MISTAKE DID THE ASTRONAUT MAKE?

He didn't consider the gravity of his situation.

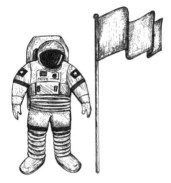

HOW DO YOU PREPARE FOR A TRIP TO MARS?

Plan-et well.

ARE ASTRONAUTS AS SMART AS THEY SAY?

For the most part, but they can be a bit
space-y.

HOW DID MARS TAKE VENUS TO COURT?

It filed a space suit.

HOW DO YOU GET A SPACESHIP TO SLEEP?

You rock-et.

WHAT'S A GOOD NAME FOR A MOLECULE?

Adam.

WHAT'S A GOOD NAME FOR A BEACH?

Sandy.

WHAT'S A GOOD NAME FOR A CHURCH?

Abby.

WHAT'S A GOOD NAME FOR A MUSEUM?

Art.

WHAT'S A GOOD NAME FOR THE EXERCISE ROOM IN A HOTEL?

Jim.

WHY DID THE VOLKSWAGEN GO TO THE HOSPITAL?

It had a bug.

WHAT IS THE BEST THING TO WEAR TO A COFFEE BAR?

A tea-shirt.

WHY DO TRAVEL REPORTERS LIKE TO GO TO LOCAL ICE CREAM PARLORS?

Because that's where they get their scoops.

WHAT IS THE CLEANEST CITY IN ENGLAND?

Bath.

HOW DO YOU CATCH A STREET?

You corner it.

WHAT DO YOU CALL A LONDON POLICEMAN?

Bobby.

WHAT DO TIRED, SLEEPY NEW YORKERS KNIT WITH?

Yawn.

HOW DO PIECES OF BREAD IN PARIS CELEBRATE?

They make a French toast.

WHERE IS THE BEST PLACE TO CELEBRATE THANKSGIVING?

Turkey.

WHERE IS THE BEST PLACE TO BUY FANCY PLATES?

China.

WHAT'S THE MOST POPULAR HOLIDAY IN EGYPT?

Mummy's Day.

IN WHAT COUNTRY DO YOU ALWAYS NEED A SWEATER?

Chile.

WHAT FLAVOR YOGURT GROWS IN THE MIDWESTERN UNITED STATES?

Plain.

WHERE DO SHARKS GO ON VACATION?

Finland.

WHAT DO HAWAIIAN COWS WEAR TO GO OUT DANCING?

Moo moos.

WHAT PEOPLE WALK VERY FAST?

Russians.

WHERE DO GIANT SEA CREATURES LIVE?

In Wales.

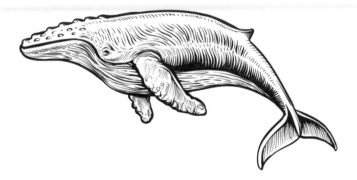

WHAT'S A GOOD NAME FOR A GERMAN MOTORCYCLIST?

Helmut.

WHAT'S A GOOD NAME FOR A HIGHWAY?

Miles.

WHAT'S THE MOST IMPORTANT MEAL OF THE DAY FOR A CAR?

Brake-fast.

WHY DID THE CAR PULL OVER TO THE SIDE OF THE ROAD?

It was tire-d.

ARE CARS FASCINATING?

Yes, they're wheely, wheely interesting.

WHAT BOAT IS ALWAYS SORRY FOR ITSELF?

A woe-boat.

HOW DOES THE ABOMINABLE SNOWMAN COMMUTE?

On an ice-cycle.

DID THE BICYCLE REALLY WIN THE DEBATE?

Nope, it spoke too soon.

WHAT SCOOTER IS ALWAYS DEPRESSED?

A mope-ed.

WHY DO PASSENGERS LIKE SHOPPING ON THEIR SHIP?

Because everything is on sail.

WHY DID THE TRAIN GET FIRED ON ITS FIRST DAY OF WORK?

It got off on the wrong track.

CHAPTER 6

SCHOOL

DID THE PLASTIC SURGEON GRADUATE FROM HIGH SCHOOL?

Yep. And then she went to collage-n.

HOW DOES A TELEVISION TEACH A CLASS?

Via remote learning.

WHAT'S THE SMARTEST VESSEL ON THE SEA?

The scholarship.

SON: "DAD, I'M BUMMED CUZ I CAN'T FIND A DATE FOR THE PROM..."

DAD: "Well, why not just look it up on the calendar?"

WHAT WAS YOUR DAD'S FAVORITE SUBJECT IN SCHOOL?

Ameripun History.

WHY DID THE HAMSTER GET TO SIT IN THE FRONT ROW OF CLASS?

It was the teacher's pet.

HOW DO YOU LEARN ABOUT PLANTS THAT WEAR LINGERIE?

You study Algae-bra.

WHAT DO YOU PAY GO TO BALLET SCHOOL?

Tu-tu-ition.

WHAT RELATIVES WILL HELP YOU WITH YOUR ENGLISH HOMEWORK?

Grammar and Grampa.

WHAT CATS GET EXPELLED FROM SCHOOL?

The Cheetah.

WHAT DO SCHOOL CROSSING GUARDS SIT ON?

An inter-sectional sofa.

WAITER: "AND WHAT WOULD YOU LIKE FOR DESSERT, SIR?"

MATH TEACHER: "I'll have the Pi à la mode, please."

WHY DIDN'T THE TEACHER CALL ON THE LIGHT BULB FOR ANSWERS?

Because it was a bit dim.

HOW CAN YOU GET YOUR BALLPOINT PEN TO MARCH?

Yell "Left! Write! Left, write, left!"

WHAT'S BEST TO WRITE WITH?

It de-pens.

WHAT GRADE DID THE EYEBALL GET IN MATH THIS YEAR?

C.

WHAT CLASS DO SNAKES TEACH AT SCHOOL?

Hiss-tory.

WHAT IS THE BEST TOOL IN THE CLASSROOM?

The scissors . . . they're a cut above the rest.

WHAT'S YOUR TEACHER'S FAVORITE DESSERT?

Chalk-o-late cake.

WHERE CAN TODDLERS PLANT FLOWERS AT SCHOOL?

In the kinder-garden.

HOW DO OMELETS GET INTO SCHOOL?

They have to pass an egg-zam.

WHY ARE PRISONERS GOOD AT BIOLOGY?

Because they know a lot about cells.

WHEN ARE TEACHERS MOST ANNOYING?

When they get test-y.

WHEN ARE TEACHERS AWESOME?

When they have a lot of class.

WHY DID THE BRUSH GET GROUNDED?

Because she didn't comb home by her curfew.

WHAT HAPPENS WHEN A CARTOON CHARACTER GETS IN TROUBLE AT SCHOOL?

Suspended animation.

WHERE DO YOU GO TO STUDY ART?

Collage.

WHAT DO FUTURE BANKERS LOVE MOST IN SCHOOL?

Show 'n' teller.

WHERE IN SCHOOL ARE YOU MOST LIKELY TO CATCH A COLD?

In the cough-ateria.

WHAT DO TREES USE TO TAKE NOTES AT SCHOOL?

Loose-leafs.

WHAT DO BASEBALL CATCHERS GET ASSIGNED A LOT OF?

Home work.

CHAPTER 7

MUSIC

HOW DO YOU SAVE A CHOIR SINGER FROM CHOKING ON HER FOOD?

Perform the Hymn-lich Maneuver.

WHAT WAS THE SYMPHONY CONDUCTOR DOING WITH A BUNCH OF KILLER WHALES AT THE AQUARIUM?

Forming an orca-stra.

KNOCK KNOCK.

Who's there?

ARIA.

Aria who?

Aria coming to the concert with me?

WHAT MUSIC EVENT IS BAD NEWS FOR BALLOONS?

K-pop concerts.

HOW DOES A COMPOSER CELEBRATE HER BIRTHDAY?

**She blows out the candles on her
sheet cake music.**

WHAT DO YOU CALL A BUNCH OF DEPRESSED
LANDSCAPERS PLAYING BANJO?

A bluegrass band.

WHY DO CHAMBER MUSICIANS WEAR BLACK?

Because it's the dress coda, duh!

WHAT DO YOU CALL A SLOW-TEMPO BARK?

A-dogio.

WHAT MUSIC BRINGS YOU UP AND DOWN?

Elevator music.

HOW DO WOODWIND INSTRUMENTS GET POPULAR?

They become social media in-flute-ncers.

WHAT IS THE MOST DANGEROUS INSTRUMENT TO PLAY?

The Bermuda Triangle.

WHY WAS THE PIANO LOCKED OUT OF ITS HOUSE?

It lost its keys.

WHAT MUSICAL INSTRUMENTS ARE DONATED TO HOSPITALS?

Organs.

WHY DO MUSICIANS DO SO WELL IN CLASS?

Because they take lots of notes.

WHAT'S A DRUMMER'S FAVORITE PART OF A CHICKEN?

The drumstick.

DID THE DRUM WIN THE CONTEST?

No, it got beat.

WHAT PHYSICAL TRAIT IMPROVES YOUR VIOLIN PLAYING?

A clef chin.

HOW DID THE VIOLIN GET INTO THE ORCHESTRA?

It pulled some strings.

WHY WAS THE BIG VIOLIN ANNOYED WITH THE LITTLE VIOLIN?

Because it was always fiddle-ing around.

CAN YOU CLEAN YOUR TEETH WITH A MUSICAL INSTRUMENT?

Yes, use a tuba toothpaste.

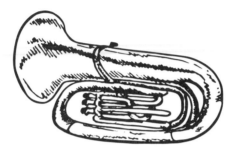

WHAT INSTRUMENT BOILS HOT WATER WHEN YOU PLAY IT?

The kettle drum.

WHAT VEGETABLE PLAYS THE DRUMS IN A ROCK BAND?

The beet.

WHAT SEAFOOD DISH DO SAXOPHONE PLAYERS EAT?

Blow-fish.

HOW DID THE TRUMPET DO WHEN HE AUDITIONED FOR THE ORCHESTRA?

He blew it.

WHY DIDN'T BILLY TOSS HIS KID SISTER IN THE AIR?

He didn't want to harm-Monica.

WHY WAS THE CELLO SO UPSET?

It was only making a bass salary.

WHICH PANTS MAKE BEAUTIFUL MUSIC?

Bell bottoms.

WHAT INSTRUMENT DO DOGS PLAY?

The trom-bone.

WHAT INSTRUMENT IS IDEAL FOR SHOPPING AT THE MALL?

Bag-pipes.

WHAT DID THE PICCOLO'S MOTHER TELL HER CHILD?

"Don't piccolo your nose!"

CHAPTER 8

MOTHER NATURE

WHERE DO PLANTS SUNBATHE?

Oh, any patio fern-ature will do.

WHAT CAUSES A TORNADO OF LEAFY GREEN VEGETABLES?

Kale force winds.

WHAT SHOULD YOU PACK FOR A CAMPING TRIP IN THE WOODS?

Toiletrees.

WHY DID THE BOTANIST LOSE ALL HIS TEETH?

Because he had bad floral hygiene.

WHAT IS MOTHER NATURE'S FAVORITE DOLLY PARTON SONG?

Gaia Will Always Love You.

HOW DID THE ANCIENT GREEKS TAKE CARE OF THE PLANET?

They did a lot of re-cyclops-ing.

HOW DOES THE SUN SAY HELLO?

It gives you a heatwave.

AND HOW DOES THE MOON SAY HELLO?

It gives you a tidal wave.

WHAT DID THE OLD MAN DO WHEN HE LOST HIS CANE IN A STORM WHILE WALKING WITH HIS WIFE?

He borrowed hurri-cane.

WHAT WEATHER PHENOMENON KNOCKS DOWN SOCIAL MEDIA PLATFORMS IN AN INSTANT?

An avatar-nado.

HOW DID FARMERS PASS THE TIME IN THE 1930S?

They joined the Dust Bowl-ing League.

IS IT GONNA RAIN ANY TIME SOON?

I highly drought it.

WHY DID THE TREE TRAVEL TO HIS HOMETOWN?

He was searching for his roots.

WHY DID THE TREE'S BIRTHDAY PARTY END SO EARLY?

The other trees started leaf-ing.

WHY DID THE BOY GO TO FORESTRY CAMP?

He thought it wood be fun.

WHY ARE MOVIES ABOUT TREES SO SILLY?

The story lines are always sap-py.

WHAT'S THE SADDEST TREE OF ALL?

The weeping willow.

WHY DID THE TREE SIGN UP FOR EXTRA CLASSES?

It needed to branch out.

WHAT DID NOAH USE ON THE ARK TO HELP HIM SEE AT NIGHT?

Flood-lights.

WHAT'S A GOOD NAME FOR A POND?

Lily.

WHY DID THE FLOWER ENTER THE PAGEANT?

She was a bud-ding beauty.

IS THE SOIL ON SALE AT THE NURSERY?

Yep, and it's dirt cheap!

WHAT CANDY DO YOU FIND IN SWAMPS?

Marsh-mallows.

WHERE DOES WATER SLEEP?

In a river bed.

WHERE DO THEY AUCTION OFF BODIES OF WATER?

On e-Bay.

WHAT CARD GAME DO YOU PLAY OVER A RIVER?

Bridge.

WHAT WEATHER DO KINGS LOVE?

Reign.

WHAT WEATHER DO HORSES DISLIKE?

Rein.

DID THE FARMER THINK THERE WOULD BE ENOUGH RAIN?

He had his droughts.

WHAT HAPPENED WHEN THE KNIFE AND SPOON TOOK A HIKE?

They came upon a fork in the road.

WHERE DO PEBBLES GO TO LISTEN TO MUSIC?

To a rock concert.

WHY IS LIGHTNING SO HARD TO CATCH?

Because it bolts.

WHAT'S A GOOD NAME FOR A VOLCANO?

Ash-ley.

WHEN IS THE STORM COMING?

Monsoon-er or later.

WHAT'S A TORNADO'S FAVORITE GAME?

Twister.

WHICH NATURAL DISASTER SHOWS YOU LOTS OF PLACES AROUND TOWN?

A tour-nado.

WHAT KIND OF STORM IS VERY SPICY?

A Thai-phoon.

WHAT KIND OF WAVE ATTACKS BOOKSTORES?

A title wave.

WHAT SHOULD YOU DO IN AN ICE STORM?

Hail a cab.

WHAT DO YOU HEAR WHEN YOU DROP AN OMELET IN THE GRAND CANYON?

Egg-o, egg-o, egg-o.

WHAT IS FROSTY THE SNOWMAN'S FAVORITE SONG?

"There snow business like show business. . . ."

WHY WON'T SOMEONE TELL YOU IF AN AVALANCHE IS COMING?

What you don't snow won't hurt you.

CHAPTER 9

SPORTS

YOGA INSTRUCTOR: "OKAY, FOLKS. CLASS IS OVER."

YOGA STUDENT: "Sooooo, should I namaste or should I go?"

HOW DOES A YOGA INSTRUCTOR PUNISH A PIRATE FOR DOING BAD YOGA?

She makes him walk the side plank.

WHAT CHAIRS ARE POPULAR AT TENNIS MATCHES?

Love seats.

WHAT WAS ANNOUNCED AT THE SCUBA DIVERS' GENDER REVEAL PARTY?

That they were having twins—both a buoy and a girl!

WHAT EXERCISE TAKES THE LONGEST AT THE GYM DURING PEAK HOURS?

Wait lifting.

HOW DID THE SKI INSTRUCTOR GET TO THE TOP OF THE MOUNTAIN?

He got a lift.

WHAT'S THE NEW OLYMPICS MOTTO?

If at first you don't succeed, tri-athlon again.

WHAT DOES A JUDGE ISSUE IF YOU BREAK THE LAW AT A GYM?

A bench press warrant.

HOW DOES A GARDENER WIN AT GOLF?

She makes a hoe-in-one.

WHAT HAPPENED TO THE MORTICIAN CLIMBING MOUNT EVEREST?

He got severe formaldehydration.

WHAT ATHLETES ALWAYS END UP IN COURT?

Tennis players.

AND WHY DO THEY END UP THERE?

They get served.

WHEN SHOULD CHEERLEADERS CARRY FIRE EXTINGUISHERS?

Whenever they do a pyro-mid.

WHAT DO YOU CALL A CHESS GAME THAT GETS VIOLENT?

A pawn-tact sport.

HOW CAN YOU TELL A YOGA INSTRUCTOR IS CONCERNED?

He's in Worrier Pose.

WHY DID THE SKYDIVING INSTRUCTOR KEEP REPEATING HIMSELF?

He was wearing a parrot-chute.

WHAT SPORT ARE LITERARY COWBOYS GREAT AT?

Bull-writing.

WHAT MARTIAL ARTS DO HIPPIES PRACTICE?

Tie-dye chi.

HOW DO YOU ADOPT A BILLIARD TABLE?

Start with the res-cue ball.

MOUNTAIN CLIMBER #1: "YOU LOOK EXHAUSTED. MAYBE YOU SHOULD TAKE A BREAK BEFORE WE SUMMIT?"

**Mountain Climber #2: "Nah, let's keep goin'.
I don't Everest."**

WHAT OUTDOOR SPORT CAUSES SKIN GROWTHS?

White wart-er rafting.

WHY WAS THE INSECT SUCH A BAD BASEBALL PLAYER?

It kept hitting fly-balls.

WHY IS BASEBALL THE RICHEST SPORT?

It's the only one played on a diamond.

HOW DO YOU GET WATER AT A BASEBALL GAME?

Ask for a pitcher.

HOW DOES A CHEF CATCH A BASEBALL?

With an oven mitt.

WHAT SPORT MAKES A LOT OF NOISE AT NIGHT?

Cricket.

WHAT SPORTS DO NEARSIGHTED PEOPLE PLAY?

Contact sports.

WHY WAS THE TENNIS PLAYER TOLD TO QUIET DOWN?

He was making a racket.

WHAT KIND OF RAFT MELTS IN WATER?

An ice cream float.

HOW DO YOU DECORATE A ROWBOAT FOR CHRISTMAS?

You hang oar-naments on it.

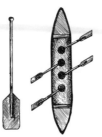

WHAT TYPE OF SHIRT SHOULD ROWERS ON A BOAT WEAR?

A crew neck.

WHAT BOATS TALK TOO MUCH?

Kay-yaks.

WHY DO PEOPLE ENJOY FISHING SO MUCH?

It's a sport you can really get hooked on.

WHAT DID THE SCUBA DIVER SAY WHEN HE WAS GIVEN MORE AIR?

"Tanks!"

WHY ARE COUCHES GOOD TO BUNGEE-JUMP WITH?

They cushion your fall.

WHY ARE ROLLER BLADES GOOD TO USE?

Because they keep you in-line.

WHAT'S THE BEST SEASON FOR SKYDIVING?

Fall.

WHAT SPORT DO TRAINS SIGN UP FOR AT SCHOOL?

Track and field.

WHAT'S SO GREAT ABOUT RUNNING MARATHONS?

They jog your memory.

WHAT EARRINGS DO BASKETBALL PLAYERS WEAR?

Hoops.

WHAT SPORT IS PLAYED ON A CARPET?

Rug-by.

WHAT SPORT IS PLAYED IN BETWEEN TWO MOUNTAINS?

Valley-ball.

WHAT KIND OF PARTIES DO SHOES ATTEND?

Foot-balls.

WHY DID THE FOOTBALL PLAYER BUY A LAWN MOWER?

He had a lot of yards to go.

WHAT DID THE FOOTBALL COACH YELL WHEN THE TELEPHONE DIDN'T RETURN HIS MONEY?

"Hey! I want my quarter back!"

WHAT SNACK DO DUCKS SERVE AT SUPER BOWL PARTIES?

Quackers and cheese.

WHAT DO GOLFERS WEAR AT TOURNAMENTS?

Tee shirts.

HOW DO YOU LEARN TO PLAY GOLF?

Take a golf course.

WHAT'S A GOLFER'S FAVORITE LUNCH?

A club sandwich.

WHAT HAPPENS WHEN GOLFERS GOSSIP?

They can be very caddy.

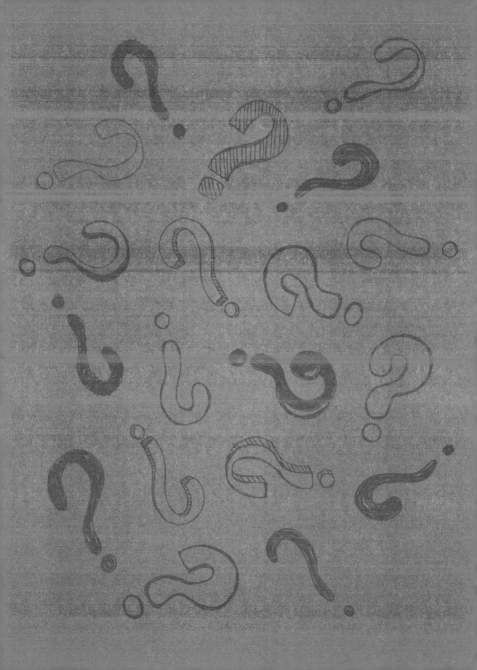

CHAPTER 10

MISCELLANEOUS

WHERE DO GEORGE WASHINGTON, THOMAS JEFFERSON, JOHN ADAMS, BENJAMIN FRANKLIN, ALEXANDER HAMILTON, JOHN JAY, AND JAMES MADISON GO FOR REUNIONS?

The Lost & Founding Fathers.

WHAT DOES THE SUCCESS OF CLAUDE MONET IN THE ART WORLD MEAN?

That first impressionists matter.

WHAT DOES STARBUCKS CHARGE YOU IF YOU HAVE A COLD?

A cough-fee.

WHAT DID THE PHILOSOPHER TELL HIS CHILDREN AT SUPPER?

"Remember, kids, no dessert until you've eaten everything on your Plato."

HOW DOES CHARLES DARWIN ENTER A BUILDING?

He goes through the evolving door.

WHAT DO FRENCH PHILOSOPHERS PUT THEIR GROCERIES IN?

In shopping Des-cartes.

WHAT'S A GOOD NAME FOR A DENIM JACKET?

Jean.

WHAT DO SCIENTISTS WEAR TO THE LAB?

Sneakers with test tube socks.

WHAT DO YOU CALL THE MARRIAGE OF TWO OLD SOCKS?

Hole-y matrimony.

WHAT KIND OF MUSIC DO SHOEMAKERS LOVE?

Sole music.

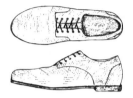

HOW DID THE SHOE SALESMAN GET HIS DAUGHTER INTO THE MOVIE WITHOUT PAYING?

He had to sneaker in.

WHY DID THE COWBOY LEAVE HIS JOB AT THE SHOE STORE?

He got the boot.

WHAT DOES A PHONE BOOK WEAR TO A FANCY PARTY?

Ad-dress.

WHAT DO YOUR CLOTHES DO WHEN YOUR CLOSET IS TOO FULL?

Oh, they just hang around.

WHAT NUTRIENT DO CLOTHES NEED?

Iron.

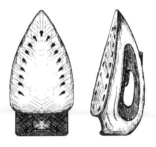

WHY DID THE SKIRT END UP IN PRISON?

It pleated guilty.

WHERE DO FINGER PUPPETS GET THEIR OUTFITS?

They're all hand-me-downs.

WHAT UNDERWEAR DO PRIZEFIGHTERS WEAR?

Boxer shorts.

HOW DO YOU KNOW A HAT IS IN A GOOD MOOD?

It's brim-ming with joy.

WHY DID THE HAT TURN BAD?

It was hanging out with a lot of hoods.

HOW DO YOU ENTERTAIN A HEMLINE?

Keep it in stitches.

WHY WERE THE PANTS BROUGHT TO THE POLICE PRECINCT?

They got cuffed.

WHAT DID THE MOTHER SAY TO THE BOOK BEFORE IT WENT OUTSIDE TO PLAY?

"Don't forget to put on your jacket!"

HOW DID ONE MITTEN FEEL ABOUT THE OTHER MITTEN?

He was in glove with her.

WHAT JACKETS DO FIREFIGHTERS WEAR?

Blaze-ers.

WHAT IS A TIE'S FAVORITE SHAKESPEAREAN QUOTE?

"To be or knot to be."

WHAT'S A NICE GIFT TO GIVE A PASTRY CHEF?

Flours.

WHERE DO FLOUR AND EGGS MEET?

At a mixer.

WHAT HAPPENED WHEN THE PANCAKE MET THE SPATULA?

She flipped for him.

HOW DID CRITICS RATE THE NEW COOKING SHOW ON TV?

They pan-ned it.

WHY DID THE STOVE QUIT ITS JOB?

It got burned out.

HOW DID THE COPS GET THE SAUSAGE TO CONFESS?

They kept grilling it.

WHAT UTENSILS DO CONSTRUCTION WORKERS EAT WITH?

Fork lifts.

WHAT DO FOOTBALL LINEBACKERS EAT CEREAL FROM?

A super-bowl.

WHY ARE REFRIGERATORS HARD TO MAKE FRIENDS WITH?

Because they're very cool customers.

WHY WAS THE STICK OF DEODORANT SO DEPRESSED?

Its life was the pits.

WHERE DID THE DIRT TAKE HIS DATE?

To the dust-ball.

WHY DID THE LOAD OF LAUNDRY QUIT ITS JOB?

Its career was all washed up.

WHAT KIND OF BIKE DOES A WASHING MACHINE RIDE?

A spin cycle.

KID: DAD, WHY ARE PEOPLE SO FUSSY ABOUT THEIR SHAMPOO?

DAD: Because it's hair today, gone tomorrow.

WHY WAS THE TOILET PAPER HAVING SUCH GOOD LUCK?

It was on a roll.

WHERE ARE REFRIGERATORS BUILT?

In Chile.

WHY IS IT SO TIRESOME TO FIX A BROKEN SHOWER?

The work is very drain-ing.

HOW CAN YOU TELL THAT A TOILET BOWL IS EMBARRASSED?

It gets all flushed.

WHAT'S A GOOD NAME FOR A BATHROOM RUG?

Matt.

HOW DO RABBITS KEEP THEIR HAIR IN GOOD SHAPE?

With a hare conditioner.

WHAT KIND OF MAIL DO AIR CONDITIONERS RECEIVE?

Fan mail.

WHY DID THE SPONGE QUIT HIS JOB?

His career was all dried up.

WHY WAS THE FAUCET SO WORRIED?

It had a sink-ing feeling.

WHAT MAKES TOWELS SO FUNNY?

They have a dry sense of humor.

HOW DO MIRRORS PASS THE TIME?

Reflecting on the passing scene.

ARE RAZORS SMART?

Yes, they're very sharp.

WHY DON'T LAMPS GET SUNBURNED?

Because they're always in the shade.

WHY DON'T DOORS LIKE TO PLAY WITH WINDOWS?

Because windows are a pane in the neck.

HOW DOES A WINDOW GET CHOSEN FOR A HOUSE?

It has to be screened for the job.

WHAT DO THE LIBRARY POLICE DO?

They book people.

HOW DO BABIES CHEAT ON TESTS?

They use crib notes.

WHAT SHOULD YOU SIT ON AT A ROCK CONCERT?

A rockin' chair.

WHAT FURNITURE HELPS YOU DO YOUR MATH HOMEWORK?

A count-er.

WHAT'S A GOOD NAME FOR A MATTRESS?

Bette.

WHAT DID THE PILLOW SAY TO THE CRYING COMFORTER?

"Why are you so down?"

WHAT FURNITURE IS SELDOM SEEN IN PUBLIC?

Your drawers.

WHAT VEGETABLE WATCHES TOO MUCH TELEVISION?

A couch potato.

WHAT KIND OF CHAIR WEARS A BRACELET?

An arm chair.

WHAT IS THE OLDEST PIECE OF FURNITURE IN THE HOUSE?

The grandfather clock.

WHAT'S A CLOCK'S FAVORITE GAME?

Tick-Tock-Toe.

WHAT HAPPENED WHEN THE PICNIC TABLE PLAYED BASKETBALL?

It got bench-ed.

TOMMY: HEY, BILL, HOW MUCH VOLTAGE IS IN A LIGHT BULB?

BILL: Watt does it matter?

WHY WAS THE DAUGHTER MAILBOX MAD AT THE DADDY MAILBOX?

Because he wouldn't let-ter go to the mall.

IMAGE CREDITS

34 top; Gulnara Khadeeva: 82, 83; Koshevnyk: 154; LAATA9: 177; lawang design: 26 top, 35 bottom; Natalya Levish: 46 top, 47; Lidok_L: 70 bottom; logaryphmic: 52; Yevheniia Lytvynovych: 58 bottom; Kate Macate: 48; MaKars: 22, 94, 96 top, 125; Marylia: 79; Aleks Melnik: 19 bottom, 7, 8, 9, 10, 11, 12, 16, 51 bottom, 69 bottom, 78, 87, 151, 159; Melok: 104; melonee: 137; mhatzapa: 124; Nadezhda Molkentin: 42, 43, 133 top; moopsi: 60 top; N.Petrosyan: 37; nadiia_oborska: 180 bottom; Natchapol18: 49; Net Vector: 178 top; Netkoff: 64, 65, 76 bottom; nikiteev_konstantin: 103, 166; Sergey Nivens: 152 top; pilotv: 2; Pylypchuk: 144; Pinchuk Oleksandra: 69 top; Qualit Design: 136; Random Illustrator: 40 top; Alexandra Romanova: 132; rraya: 54; Rumdecor: 130, 131; Marina Santiaga: 30, 32 top; SAXANA-art: 88 top; schwarzhana: 95 top; Ecaterina Scuichina: 24, 25; ShustrikS: 128; simpleBE: 23, 36 bottom, 41 bottom; Spicy Truffle: 181; Helen Stebakov: 38; SuperArt Works: 55 bottom; svetalik: 92 bottom; tapilipa: 126 bottom; Travel Drawn: 160; tsaplia: 86; Olha Turchenko: 13 bottom, 50 top, 51 top, 57, 112 top, 167, 174, 178 bottom, 182; una_llenella: 13 top; Vasilyeva Larisa: 85; Vectorgoods studio: 27; vectorsws: 89; vitdes: 70, 99; VladisChern: 127; white snow: 56; Vlada Young: 96 bottom; Olena Zhdanovskykh: 112 bottom

Courtesy of Wikimedia Commons/Pearson Scott Foresman: 6, 28 bottom, 29, 33 top, 34 bottom, 35 top, 75 top